Writing Activities for the AB Star

These **45** activities accompany the Jelly and Bean books 1 to 4 in the **A Series** and books 1 to 4 in the **B Series**. These books are available as the **AB Starter Pack**.

The activities provide comprehensive practice for reading and writing simple words made up of 18 of the letters introduced in Phonic Phase 2 of *Letters and Sounds*. The letters used are 'a, b, c, d, e, f, g, h, i, l, m, n, o, p, r, s, t, u'. The letter 'k/k' is not used in the Starter Pack.

The high-frequency words introduced are *a, on* in books 1A and 1B, *in, big* in books 2A and 2B, *and* in books 2B, 3A and 3B, and *the* in books 4A and 4B.

There are no capital letters, verbs or sentences in any of the activities.

Handwriting the letters

The letters in this book have all been printed using the Sassoon Infant typeface. This font aims to teach children the hand movements associated with the writing of each letter of the alphabet.

The letters are grouped together in the same way as the DfEE publications 'Developing Early Writing' (2001), and 'Letters and Sounds' (2007).

c a d o g q e all begin with an anticlockwise movement of the hand.

m n h b p r k begin with a downward movement of the hand which is then retraced upward and followed by a clockwise movement.

t l u i j y begin with a downward movement of the hand followed by a turn at the bottom of the stroke.

s f begin with an anticlockwise movement followed by a clockwise movement.

v w x z k use straight lines only.

The letters q j k k y v w z are not used in the activities in this book.

Marlene Greenwood © 2015

Contents

c o a t

h n m i

b g d f

l r s e

u p x

Name..

Write over the dotted letters.
Write the words by yourself on the dotted line.

c c c c t t t

a a a a a a

h h h h

cat   hat

....

Name..

Draw a line from each word to the correct picture.

Write over the dotted letters. Write each word by yourself.

hat

....

mat

cat

....

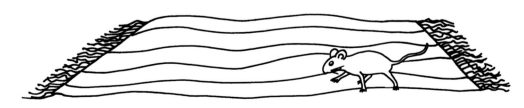

Name..

Write the correct words under each picture.

| a hat | a mat | a cat |

Practise writing the letters.

h   h   h

....

m   m   m

t   t   t

....

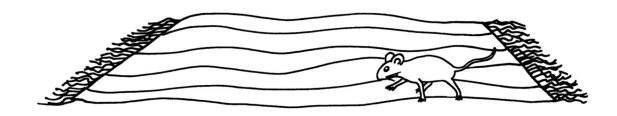

a   a   a

Name..

Draw a line from each phrase to the correct picture. Write

the words **cat hat mat on a** on the lines.

....

a mat on a cat

....

....

a cat on a mat

a hat on a mat	....

....

Writing activities from Jelly and Bean

Name..

Write over the dotted letters.
Then write the words by yourself.

o   o   o   o   o   o

n   n   n   n   n   n

cot

can

....

....

Writing activities from Jelly and Bean

Name..

Write over the dotted letters and words.
Write the words on the dotted lines.

a cat on a man.

a hat on a man.

....

....

Writing activities from Jelly and Bean

Name..

Draw a line from each word to the correct picture.

Write the correct word under each picture.

can

hot

cat

cot

Writing activities from Jelly and Bean

Name...

Draw a line from each word to the correct picture.
Practise the letters on the dotted lines.

m m n n h h

hat   man   mat   hot

....

....

....

Writing activities from Jelly and Bean

Name..

Write the missing letter in each word. Draw a line from each word to the correct picture. Write the words.

c t a

ca_

_ot

c_n

Writing activities from Jelly and Bean

Name..

Write over the dotted letters and words.
Write the words by yourself.

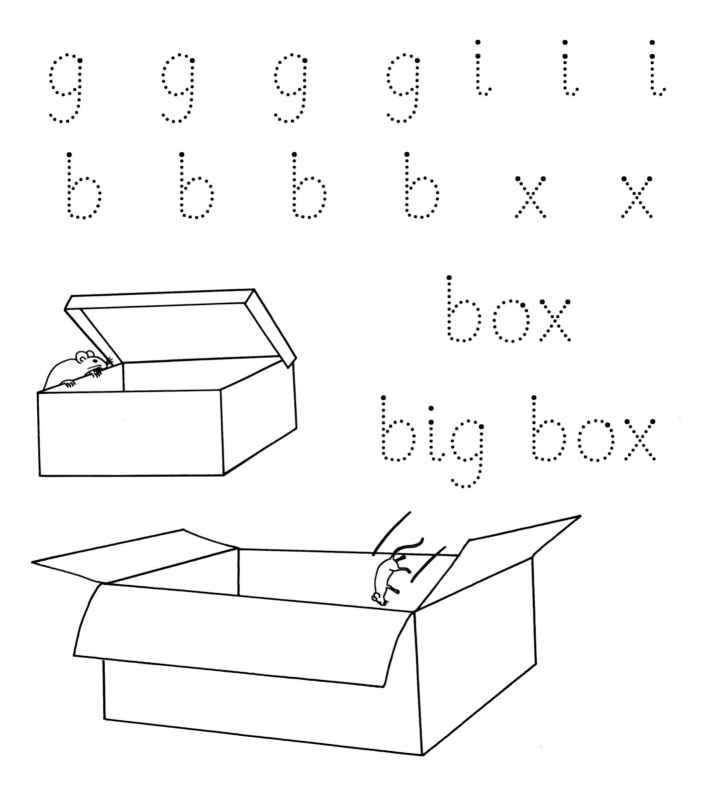

g g g g i i i

b b b b x x

box

big box

Name...

Draw a line from the words to the correct picture.

a hat in a box

a cat in a hat

a cat in a box

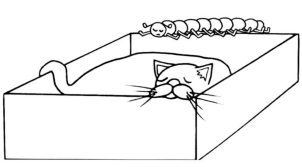

Write over the dotted words. Write the words by yourself.

hat   cat   box   in

....

....

Name...

Write the correct word in each gap.

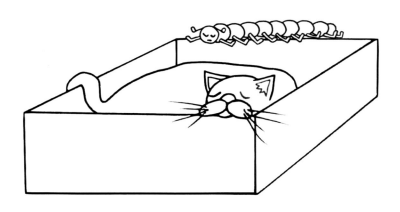

| in |
| on |

a cat .... a box

| in |
| on |

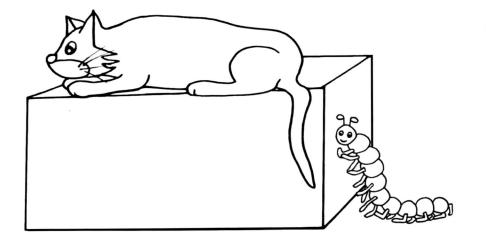

a cat .... a box

Practise writing the words below.

in ....   on ....

Writing activities from Jelly and Bean

Name...

Write **a** in each word.

Draw a line from each word to the correct picture.

c_n

m_n

c_t

b_t

h_t

Writing activities from Jelly and Bean

Name...

Practise writing the letters. Draw a line from the word to the correct picture. Write the words by yourself.

b   b   b   b   b   b

i   i   i   i   i

| b a t |

| t i n |

| b i n |

....

....

Writing activities from Jelly and Bean

Write the correct word under each picture.

| bat | bin | tin | bat |

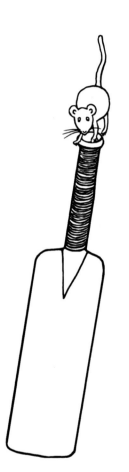

....

....

....

....

Name..

Draw a line from the words to the correct picture.
Write the dotted words on the lines.

a tin in a bin

a bat in a bin

a bat in a box

bin ....

tin ....

bat ....

box ....

Writing activities from Jelly and Bean

Name..

Write the correct letter in each word.
Draw a line from each word to the correct picture.

b x g i

_at

ba_

bo_

b_n

Writing activities from Jelly and Bean

Name...

Write over the dotted letters and words.
Then write the words by yourself.

d   d   d   d   f   f   f   f

l   l   l   l   l   r   r   r   r

frog

dog

log

....

....

    Writing activities from Jelly and Bean

Name...

Draw a line from the words to the correct picture.
Practise writing the letters and words.

a dog

a frog

a log

a dog ....

a log ....

a frog ....

Writing activities from Jelly and Bean

Name ....

Look at each picture, then write the correct word in each space.

in	on	and

a cat .... a bin

a cat .... a can

a dog .... a mat

a dog .... a bat

Writing activities from Jelly and Bean

Name..

Write over the dotted letters **b** and **d**

b   b   b   b   b   b

d   d   d   d   d   d

Write over the words, then write the words by yourself.

a bad dog

a mad bat

....

....

Writing activities from Jelly and Bean

Name...

Write over the dotted letters and words.
Then write the words by yourself.

u   u   u   u   u   u

e   e   e   e   e   e

a cat in the mud

....

....

Writing activities from Jelly and Bean

Name..

Draw a line from the words to the correct picture.

Write the words by yourself.

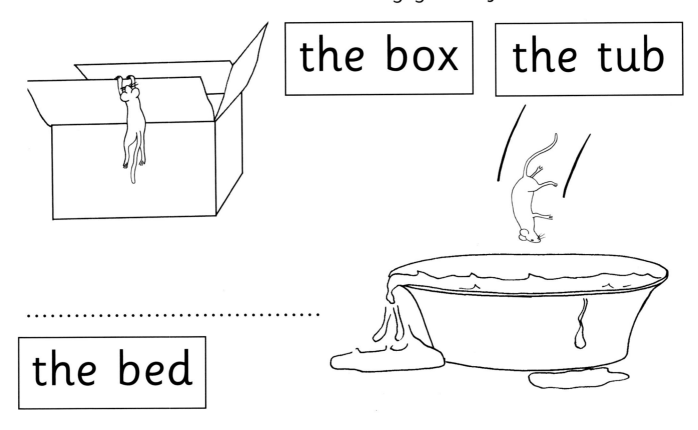

the box   the tub

the bed

....

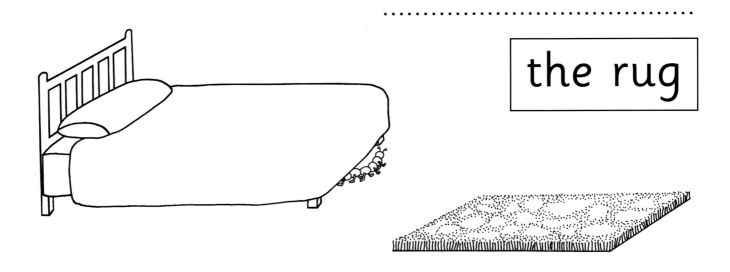

the rug

....

Name...

Draw a line from each word to the correct picture.
Practise writing the words.

s s s s s s s

cat

cats

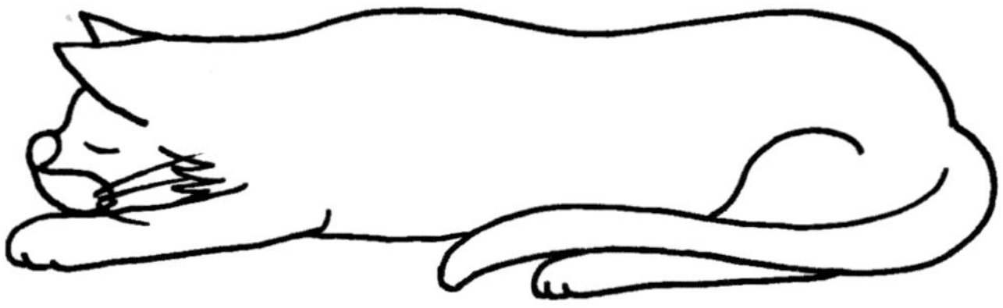

dogs

dog

....

....

Writing activities from Jelly and Bean

Name..

Draw a line from each set of words to the correct picture.
Write the dotted words by yourself.

a cat on the bed

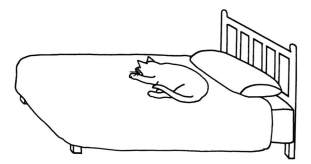

cats on the bed

cats on the rug

a cat in the mud

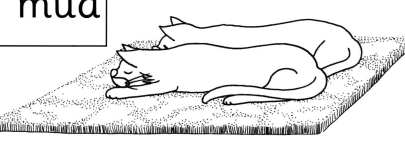

bed   mud   rug

....

Writing activities from Jelly and Bean

Name...

Practise writing **e**, then write **e** in each word.
Draw a line from each word to the correct picture.

e   e   e   e   e   e

h_n

t_n

n_t

b_d

Writing activities from Jelly and Bean

Name..

Practise writing **d.** Then writ**e** **d** in each word.

Draw a line from each word to the correct picture.

d d d d d d

_og

mu_

be_

_ot

Writing activities from Jelly and Bean

Name...

Practise writing **p**. Draw a line from each word to the correct picture. Write each word on a dotted line.

p   p   p   p   p   p

pan

cup

....

tap

pin

pop

....

....

....

    Writing activities from Jelly and Bean

Name...

Practise writing p and u Write each word under the correct picture.

p   p   p   p   p   p

u   u   u   u   u   u

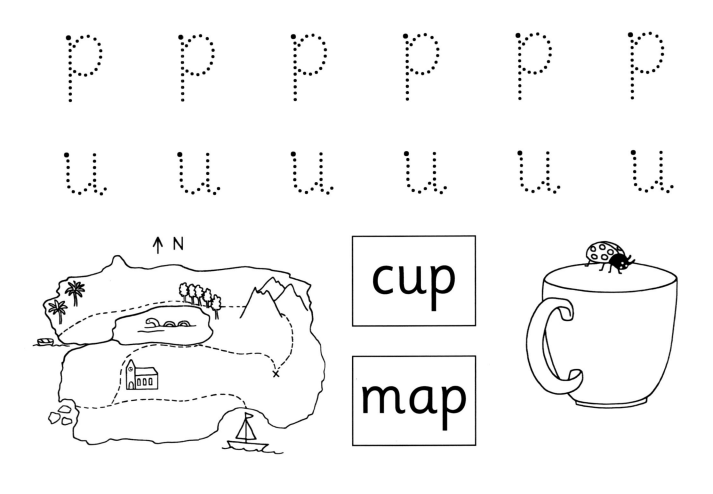

cup

map

....

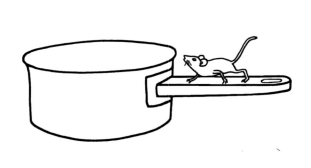

mud

pan

....

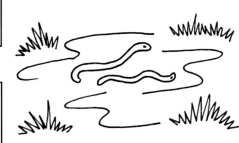

....

Writing activities from Jelly and Bean

Name..

Practise writing **b** and **p**. Write each word under the correct picture.

b   b   b   b   b   b

p   p   p   p   p   p

| bugs | bat | hop | pet |

....

Name..

Draw a line from each picture to the correct words.

| a bad dog |
| a mad cat |
| a hot pan |
| a pet rabbit |

Write a word with **b** in it ....

Write a word with **d** in it ....

Write a word with **p** in it ....

Writing activities from Jelly and Bean

Name..

Draw a line from each picture to the correct words.

Practise writing the word **the.**

the the the

....

the big box

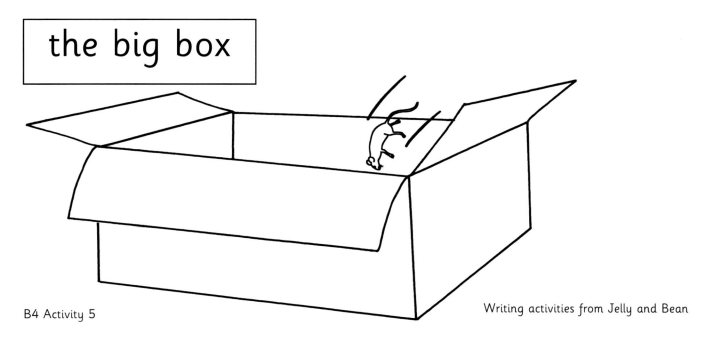

Writing activities from Jelly and Bean

Name..

Write **m** in each word.

Draw a line from each word to the correct picture.

_an

_ug

_ap

_at

Writing activities from Jelly and Bean

Name..

Write **i** in each word.

Draw a line from each word to the correct picture.

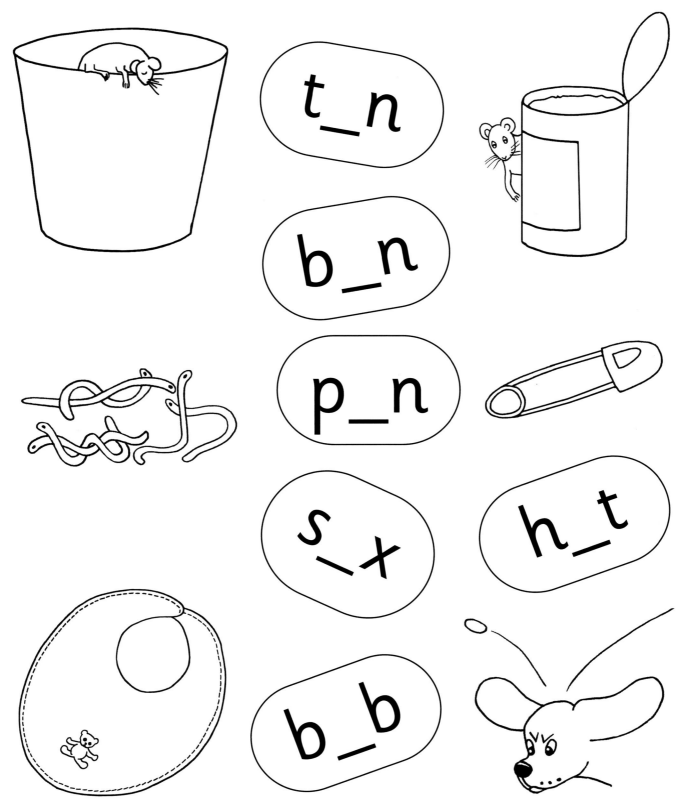

t_n

b_n

p_n

s_x

h_t

b_b

Writing activities from Jelly and Bean

Name...

Write **u** in each word.

Draw a line from each word to the correct picture.

b_gs

c_p

r_g

t_b

m_d

Writing activities from Jelly and Bean

Name..

Write n in each word.

Draw a line from each word to the correct picture.

_et

ca_

ti_

he_

te_

Writing activities from Jelly and Bean

Name..

Write **t** in each word.

Draw a line from each word to the correct picture.

_ap

ho_

ne_

ba_

hi_

ha_

Writing activities from Jelly and Bean

Name...

Write **h** in each word.

Draw a line from each word to the correct picture.

_op

_at

_it

_ot

_en

Writing activities from Jelly and Bean

Name...

Write **r** in each word.

Draw a line from each word to the correct picture.

f_og

_at

_abbit

_ug

Writing activities from Jelly and Bean

Name..

Write the missing letter in each word.
Draw a line from each word to the correct picture.

s f r l

_un

_at

_rog

_og

Writing activities from Jelly and Bean

Name...

Write the correct phrase under each picture.

the cat and the bat

the bugs in the mud

....

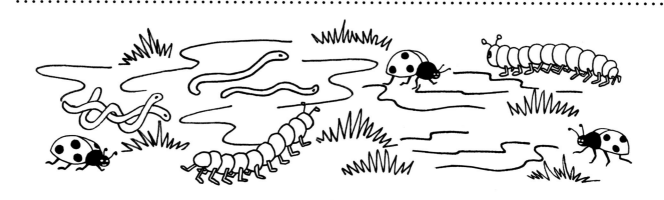

....

Writing activities from Jelly and Bean